Made with Love

By

....

INTRODUCTION

Dear Grandad, this is a memory book where you can write your unique life story and precious moments of your life based on guided questions and prompts.

It's your chance to inspire your grandchildren with your life experience and achievements. besides, of course being their grandfather, you will be a source of inspiration to them.

Skip any questions that might not be relevant to you at the moment and if you need to sticking in photos and other mementos for a special occasion there are extra pages at the back.

Then have fun filling this book and give to your Grandchild

TABLE OF CONTENTS

ON THE DAY YOU WERE BORN

Full name: ____

Time of Birth: ____

Weight: ____

Height: ____

Hair Color: ____

ON THE DAY YOU WERE BORN

Day of the week: ____

The weather: ____

#1 Song: ____

#1 Movie: ____

#1 Book: ____

Famous People who share your birthday: ______________________________

____

____

Zodiac: ____

Birthstone: ____

World Population: ____

Most popular baby names this year: __________________________________

____

Historical Events: ____

____

____

When and where were you born?

How did your parents choose your name? Did you have any nicknames?

Did your parents tell you anything about the day you were born

Tell me about your parents. Where were they born? When were they born?

What were the occupations of your parents?

What do you remember most about your mother?

What do you remember most about your father?

Who was more strict: your mother or your father? Do you have a vivid memory of something you did that you were disciplined for?

What do you remember most about your grandparents?

Do you remember any of the stories they used to tell you?

How many brothers and sisters do you have? When were they born?

Could you tell me a story or a special memory
about your brothers and sisters?

What interesting stories do you know about other people in your family?

Did you have a pet growing up? What were their names

Where did you live as a child? What are the earliest memories about your Childhood home?

How did your family earn money? How did your family compare to others in the neighborhood – richer, poorer, the same?

What kinds of things did your family spend money on?

What family trip do you remember most

What is the funniest family story you remember?

Do you have any favorite family recipes?

Are there any fun family legends and stories about people from older generations?

Where did our ancestors come from?

What was your Christmas/Hanukkah/Holidays like growing up

Who were your favorite relatives?

What do you remember most about your childhood?

What were your favorite toys as a kid? What games did you play?

What kind of books did you like to read?

Did you have holidays as a child and what do you remember about them?

Tell me about your friends when you were a child.
Who was your best friend?

Tell me an interesting or funny story about your childhood?

What was your favourite television show as a child?

What did you want to be when you grew up?

Did you ever get into trouble as a child?

What did you eat when you were a child?

Did you have any child hood diseases?

Were there any similarities between me and you as a child?

Did you still have the same childhood friends growing up?

What schools did you go to? Did you enjoy school?

What was your favourite subject at school?

What kind of student were you?

Do you remember any teachers you loved (or hated!)?

How would your classmates remember you?

Are you still friends with anyone from that time in your life?

Do you have any favorite stories from school?

What do remember about your teenage years?

What was one of your favorite shows, songs, and films as a teenager?

What sorts of clothes and activities were popular when you were a teenager

What activities have you really enjoyed as an adult?

Did you and your friends have a special place to hang out? Tell me about that?

Did you have a best friend when you were young?

How did you decide on a career?

What was your first job? How much money did you make?

Have you won any special awards or prizes as an adult?
What were they for?

What was your first car?

How many times have you been in love?

How did you meet grandma
What was your marriage proposal like?

Where was your wedding? Who was your best man?

Tell me about your wedding ceremony?

What's your favorite thing about your partner?

What is your favorite thing about being a parent?

Were you ever scared to be a parent?

Tell me about the day when my mom/dad was born?

What was the funniest thing my mom/dad did as a child?

What do you remember about when each of us was born?

What is your favorite thing about being a grand parent

Who is your favourite grandchild?

Were there any similarities between me and you as a child?

What do you want your children and grandchildren to remember about you?

What is your wish for your children/grandchildren?

What tradition of yours do you hope our family continues?

What advise were you given by your parents?

WORLD'S GREATEST DAD
HAPPY
Father's
DAY

Belief and Values

What are some values you hold?

What are your hobbies?

What is the single most memorable moment of your life?

What was the most stressful experience you every lived through?

What was the scariest thing that ever happened to you?

What you most thankful for...most proud of...

Do you practice a religion? What impact has religion had on your life?

What was a historic moment that you lived through? Can you tell me about it?

What makes you happy?

What activities did you enjoy in your free time?

Who is someone you admire? Why?

How has the world changed during your life?

What Historical Events Surprised, Scared, or Excited You?

What parts of your life helped shape you as a person?

What is different today compared to when you were younger?

What's the most trouble you've ever gotten in?

What is your most embarrassing moment?

Do you have any regrets? Why or Why not?

What was the best day in your life so far?

Is there anything left on your bucket list

What advice would you like to give me?

We all love you

Grandad

www.ingramcontent.com/pod-product-compliance
Ingram Content Group UK Ltd.
Pitfield, Milton Keynes, MK11 3LW, UK
UKHW061827190726
13853UKWH00009B/2485

9 798418 010360